The Quantum Prayer

An Inspiring Guide to Love, Healing, and Creating the Best Life Possible

Dr. Joshua Kai

Copyright © 2014 Dr. Joshua Kai

The Quantum Prayer™ Dr. Joshua Kai

Quantum Prayer™ Dr. Joshua Kai

All rights reserved.

No part of this book may be reproduced by any mechanical, photographic, or electronic process, or in the form of audio recording, nor may it be stored in a retrieval system, transmitted, or otherwise be copied for public or private use without prior written permission of the author.

The author of this book does not dispense medical advice nor prescribe the use of any technique or program as a form of treatment for physical, mental, emotional, or medical problems without the advice of a physician, either directly or indirectly. The intent of the author is only to offer information of a general nature to help you in your quest for optimal living. In the event you use any of the information in this book for yourself, the author assumes no responsibility for your actions.

ISBN-13: 978-1505565003
ISBN-10: 1505565006

DEDICATION

For Susana, the love of my life.

CONTENTS

Foreword — vii

Acknowledgments — viii

A Note from Joshua — ix

Part One

Introduction

Chapter 1	The Origin of Quantum Prayer	Pg 1
Chapter 2	Quantum Timing	Pg 5
Chapter 3	The Guidance	Pg 10

Part Two

My Year of Quantum Prayer

Chapter 4	A Fork in the Road	Pg 17
Chapter 5	High Vibrational Living	Pg 21
Chapter 6	The Amazing Authentic Self	Pg 29
Chapter 7	The Quantum Prayer	Pg 33
Chapter 8	Divine Connection	Pg 38

Part Three

Living in the New Consciousness

Chapter 9	Our New Reality	Pg 44
Chapter 10	"Cell-f" Love	Pg 47
Chapter 11	Cooperation	Pg 51
Chapter 12	Shifting Perspective to Heal	Pg 55
Chapter 13	Creative Evolution	Pg 61
Chapter 14	The New Family System	Pg 66
Chapter 15	Being vs. Striving	Pg 69
Chapter 16	Reflections in the Mirror	Pg 72
Chapter 17	Learning Through Conscious Awareness	Pg 75

Part Four

Conclusion

Chapter 18	Language and Intention	Pg 80
Chapter 19	Expanding into Ascension	Pg 84
Chapter 20	Accessing You	Pg 86

A Special Note From Susana

About the Author

Join The Quantum Prayer Movement

FOREWARD

In a clear voice, and by lovingly sharing his truth, Joshua unlocks the keys of self-transformation within each of us. Exploring in an easy to understand style, the power of positive prayer, quantum energy, healing vibrations and heaven-on-earth, the author leads us to the boundless love that only wants to serve and bless the world. Held together in the bond of oneness we are easily carried to the divine wisdom of our soul and the eternal universal truths that beckon us beyond all worldly limitations. Thank you Joshua.

Dr. Rev. Debbi Brown
Unity minister, Prayer Therapist, Spiritual Healer, Therapeutic Medium

ACKNOWLEDGMENTS

I lovingly and gratefully acknowledge all of the amazing beings of love and light that have accompanied me at various points on my life path. Family, friends, colleagues, mentors, neighbors, pet-companions, and everyone who has touched my life in one way or another. Thank each and every one of you for making me a better spiritual being through this wonderful human experience of ours.

A NOTE FROM JOSHUA

Many of us are familiar with the shifts occurring on our planet and in Humanity to ever-higher vibrational frequencies, and are now seeking to understand what these shifts will manifest for us on both a planetary level and on an individual human level.

These new higher vibrational dimensions provide access to new realities, which allow us to manifest, create our lives, and positively affect the world around us.

I've written this book to share with you this essential guidance and my own personal story to provide perspective and insight on how to utilize Quantum Prayer in your own life to manifest, create, heal, prosper, and even discover your own life purpose.

Dr. Joshua Kai

PART ONE

INTRODUCTION

> "…the deeper my connection grew to Oneness, the more I started to experience myself as also being channeled, as in someone or something else was also channeling *me*."

CHAPTER ONE

THE ORIGIN OF QUANTUM PRAYER

In order to best explain the origin of Quantum Prayer, it's helpful to start with my own personal background in the realm of metaphysics and my spiritual journey.

I was born, simply stated, a bit psychic. I believe we all have psychic intuition and that some people are just more consciously aware of their natural ability to tap into the universal grid, or that part of us that is connected to all that is. I guess I just came "out of the box" that way, so to speak, fairly aware of my connected nature.

I've spent my entire life, from early childhood, developing my psychic awareness, my intuition, my consciousness, and my connection to the Universe.

In my early childhood, I can remember a fascination with reading the Bible. I had, on occasion, been to various churches and listened to the Bible "preached" in a way that did not resonate with me at all. So, I would often take the

Bible and go for a walk in the park amongst nature, and find a secluded place where I knew I would not be disturbed, somewhere deep in the woods, and read for a while. As I sat alone on the ground, I felt surrounded by God and the infinite nature of truth.

I don't know why I was compelled to read the Bible as a child. I wasn't religious, and I was already very knowledgeable of all the complex and varied religions and beliefs in the world. I really wanted to have nothing to do with any of them. Nevertheless, on those occasions when I felt compelled to read the Bile, I would become acutely aware of a sense of remembering instead of learning or reading something for the first time. I would read for a while, then simply close the book and put it down because I sensed I already knew what it said. Although I didn't have a name for it, that was the first time I became conscious of my own true nature, my own infinite nature, and that we are far more than our mental, emotional, and physical selves.

Throughout my entire adult life, I've been learning, or remembering rather, how to align more and more with God, the Universe, and my Higher-Self. I spent a lot of time in seminars, workshops, classes, working with various groups, etc., "waking up," and becoming increasingly conscious and aware of my connection with all that is.

Somewhere in my thirties, I began to practice channeling, for which I experienced a profound resonance. At first, I began channeling the energies commonly referred to as Ascended Masters and other higher-vibrational spiritual beings. As I progressed, I connected more with what I refer to as God, the Universe, and my own Higher-Self. I've come to realize that, for me, these are all the same, and the only thing that separates us is simply our perspective—our thoughts about how we see ourselves relative to everyone and everything else. It has been through my work as a channel that I now fully understand, as much as humanly possible, that we are all truly "One."

Over the last several years, my own perspective on channeling has shifted and evolved further. I started this work of channeling, thinking of myself only as the person channeling, or the channel, if you will. However, the deeper my connection grew to Oneness, the more I started to experience myself as also being channeled, as in someone or something else was also channeling *me*.

This small shift in perspective, from being "the channel" to also being "the channeled," then opened the floodgates to an incredibly expanded awareness where I was able to access, and be accessed, for nearly any creative purpose. I quickly realized that this new dimensional reality could be utilized to manifest, create, heal, prosper, and tap into creation anywhere in the quantum realms. Thus began my work with Quantum Prayer.

Most people may already have an intuitive sense of what Quantum Prayer is and means to them, yet still might struggle to find the actual words to define it if asked. I believe that's because, in the greater reality, *nothing* is really ever new, but in fact, everything already exists in consciousness and we only think of it as "new" when it re-enters our conscious field for the first time within the context of our present life experience. In this sense, even consciousness can be thought of as being "reincarnated."

For the purpose of this book, the term "Quantum" refers to the metaphysical theory that if something is in your consciousness, it can exist. Therefore, everything can exist "at once" and in the "now" by simply becoming aware.

My own definition of "Prayer" just refers to the consciousness of *placing one's intent into the light of all creation.* I've come to believe that our intentions are key, even more so than language. Of course, the language we use is very important as well, but it's a tool used to solidify our intentions, which is the universal energy used for creation.

So if tasked to define Quantum Prayer, I would simply

say that it is *creating with our intentions through awareness of our infinite nature*. With Quantum Prayer, creation always happens and exists in the now, or the present moment. That means, what you choose to create happens instantly by simply being conscious of our infinite nature and assigning our intentions to our infinite existence.

"This concept of time is a tool used in our lower dimensional reality to learn, expand, and grow from our experiences here in this present life-space. It enables us to sort of break apart, or separate, the various components of the creative process so that we can understand how creation happens, what the process is and looks like, and what our role and the role of others is in that process."

CHAPTER TWO

QUANTUM TIMING

Quantum Prayer can seem a little out of reach, considering that our present life experience still includes the concept of time. We are so used to the idea that we have to wait for something to happen and that the creative process happens in a linear fashion, that it may be difficult to understand how something, such as healing, can manifest instantly.

I'll use the term quantum timing to explain the relationship between our current reality in the lower dimensions, where time is linear, to quantum reality in the higher dimensions, where time is not experienced as linear.

Quantum timing can be understood by looking at the process of creation. In order for something to be created, there is always an arranging or re-arranging of elements to produce the intended result. A simplified example might be, if you want to build a house, in the context of time, you would build each component and perform each task in a linear fashion until the house was complete. However, usually there is a blueprint of the intended completed design, which means that, in a way, the house is already built on paper before it gets physically built. So in its essence, the house already exists in 2-D before it manifests in 3-D, which takes time.

If you were looking to buy a new house and came across the newly built house after it was completed, then you might be driving down the street and instantly see the "For Sale" sign. Essentially, the newly built house appeared in your consciousness. The fact that its various components and stages of creation did indeed occur, you were not aware of any of that. You simply intended to buy a new house and one appeared.

If you were not intending to buy a new house, you might be driving down the same street, and although the new house is built and exists, you might not have noticed it at all. So it would not have entered into your conscious awareness and you may have driven right by it and never even noticed it. Yet the house was created and does exist, just not in your consciousness. Now I'm over-simplifying this example to demonstrate the concept of how our conscious awareness plays a role in both our linear reality and our quantum reality.

Another factor to keep in mind is the concept of free will. Using the same house example, the elements of the new house were being arranged and re-arranged while the 2-D blueprint form of the house already existed. During that creative process, the people building the house could exercise their own free will by following the blueprint exactly or deviating from the blueprint along the way. Faced with many options, perhaps even some challenges, choices are made that ultimately affect the outcome, or the end result, of the new house.

So staying with the new house example, we can see the creative process in action. First, there was intent for a new house. Then, the elements were arranged and tasks were performed to build the house. Along the way, choices and options were exercised, which resulted in the house manifesting in its ultimate form at completion. From one perspective, the house took "time" to build while all of the various components, options, and choices were being arranged and decided. This is similar to how we create our lives in the lower dimension where time is experienced as linear.

We have an intention, which is the energy that spurs the universe into activating the creative process. The Universe goes about arranging and rearranging the various components necessary to create and manifest the intention. Along the way, free will is honored, and choices, options, and challenges of those involved are all factored in to the ultimate outcome.

Nonetheless, while the Universe is busy creating on your behalf, it all seems to take time for your intentions to manifest. This concept of time is a tool used in our lower dimensional reality to learn, expand, and grow from our experiences here in this present life-space. It enables us to sort of break apart, or separate, the various components of the creative process so that we can understand how creation happens, what the process is and looks like, and what our role and the role of others is in that process.

So then, if time is part of our reality, then how can we manifest something in no time at all? That's quite an amazing aspect of where we are in our current evolutionary process in humanity. We are still operating within the context of linear time and yet we are also evolving closer and closer to the higher dimensions where time is not experienced as linear. So it's possible to actually exist within, and be conscious of, both linear and nonlinear time realities, as some of us currently are. It's just a matter of shifting your perspective to include the consciousness of operating outside the context of time. Easy, right? Well, no. Until our planet and humanity evolve fully into the higher dimensions where time is not linear, we will need to operate with time as a factor and a teacher here in our present life-space.

So time exists in our current reality. That's true. It's also true that we are evolving closer to the dimensional realities of no time. It's because we are now becoming aware of these higher dimensions and the reality of nonlinear time that we can now access the vibrational frequencies of these dimensions and manifest our intentions instantly.

The more our consciousness exists in the dimensions of nonlinear time, the easier it is to experience an instant quantum leap in creation. In fact, the more we evolve toward these higher dimensions, the more we experience creation faster and faster.

It is possible, and there are some people on our planet at this time who are able to fully engage the frequencies of nonlinear time and manifest instantly. Those people are holding that vibrational frequency here for us while humanity continues to evolve. At some point, humanity and our planet will evolve completely into nonlinear time dimensions where everything and anything can be manifest instantly.

In the meantime, humanity and our planet are progressing and evolving at a much more rapid pace. By bringing guidance to humanity through Quantum Prayer, which provides an opportunity for us to become more consciously aware, we can begin to choose to keep more of our consciousness in these higher dimensions and utilize the higher dimensional frequencies for creating.

When our consciousness is fully in nonlinear dimensions, we can create instantly. Our ability to create instantly is directly related to the proportion of our consciousness in both the linear and nonlinear dimensions. The more our consciousness is in nonlinear time, the faster we can manifest.

The key to understanding the relationship between time, no time, and the guidance being offered here is to know that, once you set an intention, the Universe instantly invokes the process of arranging and re-arranging whatever is necessary to co-create that intent. Again, this happens instantly. What we experience as time is based on what portion of our consciousness is in linear time and what portion is in nonlinear time.

If there are lessons to be learned that we can use to help expand, grow, and evolve by having our consciousness in the context of linear time, our Higher-Self may opt for that experience. Once we have learned the lesson we choose to learn, we no longer need the perspective that comes with linear time. Therefore, healing, creating, and manifesting can happen instantly.

I'm sure you will find that this simple awareness, this small shift in perspective regarding time, will allow you a level of mastery over life that also expands, grows, and heals beyond anything you may have experienced in the past. I've adopted the ideal, which I share regularly with clients in my own private practice, that *even the smallest shift in perspective can bring about the greatest healing.*

> "Our seed of light can be used to 'reset' our DNA, our energy, and any and all aspects of ourselves that we choose. That means it can be accessed for healing, manifesting, and creating."

CHAPTER THREE

THE GUIDANCE

When I'm channeling, I receive information in various ways. I get images, messages, sensations, sounds, and sometimes what appears to be outright instructions. The guidance I received that I now refer to as Quantum Prayer, came to me during my own individual channeling practice. I would say that it came to me as close to outright instructions as I've ever experienced in doing this type of work. My guess is that it came through in such a manner simply because I needed it to. I am as human as one gets and most everything is subject to my very human interpretation and perspective, which undoubtedly could easily muddy up the message.

This channeled guidance came over many private sessions where I would mostly just lay comfortably in bed alone and engage as a channel. I would often keep scattered notes and notebooks of my channeling sessions, and one day I started to realize that the information I was receiving was very, very different. This was information and guidance that I had not seen or heard before in any form. Bits and pieces of the information were familiar, but the concept on the whole, and the way it was being presented to me, seemed new, or at least presented in a new light, so to speak.

The very first concept that I was shown was the image of our self as an original "seed of light." I was shown that this original seed of light, this seed of one's self, originated as a pure and perfect seed of divine love and light. It was the first time I had seen my own self in that form. It appeared to me as a tiny but brilliant, pure, perfect seed of unconditional love and light, which contained my original "blueprint," if you will, my original divine DNA. This was the essence of me, the seed from which all incarnations, divine expressions, and unique aspects of me were born. I was shown this and saw that this "original seed of me" exists now, always has, and always will. It is the source of my infinite self. Of course, it wasn't just me that I saw. I became fully aware that each of us originated as a perfect, divine seed of love and light with our original divine DNA and our original blueprint existing always.

I was then shown that all of these perfect seeds of light were once One. One perfect divine source of love and light that separated into these seeds of light for the purpose of growing and expanding itself exponentially.

I was shown that for every seed of light, there were many incarnations, many aspects, and many unique expressions. Within the context of linear time, we can think of these in terms of past, present, future, and parallel lives. With each incarnation, we began to evolve, change, and grow. Our DNA changed with each incarnation, as did our various energy fields. Based on our decisions, options, challenges, and accumulated life experiences, our physical DNA and our energy fields continued to morph and change to manifest physically that which we were choosing. I realized that our present physical body, as we experience it in this life-space, is partly an accumulation of our own unique evolutionary process.

Then I was shown something that was new to me, at least in the way it was being presented. I was shown that it's possible to access our original seed of light for any creative purpose. Our seed of light can be used to "reset" our DNA, our energy, and any and all aspects of ourselves that we choose. That means it can be accessed for healing, manifesting, and creating. Since our present incarnation is an accumulation of our evolutionary process, we would access our seed of light to essentially clear, heal, and make changes in all of our "selves," past, present, future, and parallel. Since everything is happening at once, then that clearing, healing, and change would take place at every dimensional level of our existence and it would do so instantly.

As I was receiving and processing this incredible guidance, it occurred to me that the purpose of our evolutionary process was indeed to *evolve* and that by clearing and healing the accumulation of that process, I might somehow lose the very valuable learning, growth, and expansion acquired. The answer I received was a resounding, *No!* We could, in fact, clear the unwanted aspects and retain the growth. This is similar to the concept that, once we've learned the lesson that an illness was created to teach us, we no longer need the illness and healing can take place.

I realized that one of the main keys in this model of quantum consciousness is awareness. I like to use the example of love to explain this concept. So, for example, if you love someone and you don't tell them, then they can't do much with that information. Even though the love still exists, whether you tell them or not, if they aren't aware of your love, its not yet in their consciousness. If and when you do tell them that you love them, you are bringing that truth and information into their conscious awareness. At that point, their own free will comes into play and they can do whatever they want with that information. They can choose to ignore it, reject it, embrace it, whatever they want. But they were only able to do something with that information once they were aware of it.

This guidance is similar to the example of love I just described. It was brought into my consciousness for me to become aware of. What I do with that information is a matter of my own free will and is entirely up to me. I've chosen to share the guidance I've received in any way possible to help others. It's important to note that there really isn't any sort of ritual, process, or specific requirement needed to incorporate and use this guidance. It's simply being made available to you by way of your conscious awareness, and what you do with it is completely up to you as well.

As I continued channeling, I received more and more information directly related to the "seed of light" concept, our infinite self, and how to access and create within the context of this reality. I was shown that we could impact every aspect of our lives, even as it relates to other people, places, situations, and circumstances.

That said, we cannot interfere with other people's free will. At this level of consciousness, it's not even possible. The frequency and vibration of the consciousness in this higher dimensional realm is only love and light, nothing else. Although this love and light vibration can be brought into the conscious awareness of another person, place, situation, or circumstance, free will is still in play. Using the previous example of telling someone that you love them, if you intend to bring your love for someone into their conscious awareness, they will always have free will and the choice regarding what to do with that awareness.

You might be thinking at this point, "Well, how does this work then?" It works by the lessons we've already learned in our evolutionary process, now enhanced by our new understanding of how to operate in a higher dimensional reality. Humanity has been learning very important universal truths, such as, you attract to yourself that which you are. Also, when something doesn't work out the way you may have hoped, it's because the Universe is making room for something better (more in alignment with your Higher-Self). When you apply those valuable lessons to creating and manifesting, your intentions are already aligned with the vibration of your Highest-Self and your highest good. Imagine accessing your original seed of light, spreading that pure love and light to every incarnation of yours, every lifetime, be it past, present, parallel, or future. That love and light ripples throughout every part of you, in every lifetime, healing, manifesting, and creating on your behalf, instantly.

As I was receiving this information about the "seed of light" work, I was also receiving information on the details of what life is like in our higher dimensional reality. Many of us are aware that our planet and humanity have been in the process of a very big shift into these higher dimensional realms. Life in the fifth dimension and higher/other dimensions, operates at a different vibrational frequency than it does in the third and fourth dimensions. We actually carry forth what we've learned in these lower dimensions and leave behind that which no longer serves us. I highlight some of those changes in Part III of this book, "Living in the New Consciousness."

The information provided, which describes our new reality as we continue to evolve, reaches our consciousness by awareness. This can often feel like a very subtle sense of knowing, yet it also feels very new. When you experience that sense, that's when you can be sure that you are making a shift in consciousness that will continue to grow and expand. You can then enact your free will and begin to operate within this higher dimensional reality with greater ease and benefit.

I made the personal decision long ago to create the best life possible for myself, to use any and all gifts for my highest purpose, and to help raise consciousness in every way possible. I knew that I was being provided this guidance for a purpose and that it was to be shared with others to help with our collective evolutionary process.

You will not need to memorize any of this guidance or commit to any ritual or specific practice. That is because it is being provided within the context of the higher dimensional realities, which operate at a level of pure consciousness, love, and light. Of course, what you do with this new awareness is up to you. I know that life can be transformed to a "Heaven on Earth" reality through this new awareness, if we choose. I've done just that and I wouldn't have been able to do so without also choosing to share this with others.

PART TWO

MY YEAR OF QUANTUM PRAYER

"This was an opportunity to practice acceptance, to value life's lessons, and to grow into the person I would cherish and respect the most by choosing to move forward in love, peace, and joy."

CHAPTER FOUR

A FORK IN THE ROAD

It was the beginning of a new year and I had no idea just how new this year would be for me.

It was January 11th when I came home from work on a Friday evening to discover that my (now) ex-wife was gone. I knew something was up when I pulled into the driveway and her car was not there, and I could hear my two dogs inside the house barking frantically. I could feel the energy of what had transpired there during the day flood my senses completely.

That morning when I left for work, nothing was much different from what it had ever been. But once I was gone, she apparently packed and moved herself and her adult son out in just that single day.

When I got home, our two dogs were pacing, barking, crying, and were highly agitated like I had never seen before. Still trying to figure out the situation, I went to each one to calm them while looking around at the unusual disorder of the house.

Then I saw the plain brown envelope on the dining room table with my name written on it, and proceeded to open and read it. The card offered a brief note that basically went something like, "Thanks for everything, but I don't love you, and I'm moving on." She left no indication of where she was going or any parting sentiments or concerns about our two dogs. For whatever reason, it appeared she felt like she needed to depart in this highly dramatic way and did not wish for me to know where she was going.

I started to look around the house and realized that she took what she wanted and left everything else behind. The house was a complete wreck. There were bags of trash and personal belongings, furnishings, boxes, and piles upon piles of things left behind and scattered in every room.

As each moment came and went, my shock and panic started to quickly settle into grief. I felt like someone who had suddenly died in a car crash, had left the body, and was trying to figure out what happened.

As the days went by, I began the process of cleaning up and clearing out the aftermath of their abrupt departure and all they had left behind. I'll spare you the details, but suffice it to say, I went through the gamut of denial, anger, sadness, and then finally acceptance.

I will share that I was pleasantly surprised by how quickly the acceptance part of the process came for me. Call it experience, call it intuition, it doesn't matter. I just knew deep down inside that this was the very best thing for me, and, totally free of attachment, I could begin the next chapter in my life and create whatever I wanted for myself.

Even in those very early days after my ex-wife had left, I knew that how I dealt with the energy of that situation would have a direct and significant impact on the quality of my life moving forward. So, I chose to simply wish my dearly departed the very best life possible. I began by praying for her. Not to come back, not to change her mind, and not for any specific outcome, but just for her happiest, healthiest, and greatest life. Whatever that meant for her, I supported that wholeheartedly. It was just a simple prayer, wishing her well and for all of her highest hopes and dreams to come true. And I continued to do so every day thereafter.

Now, it was like a fork in the road that I could clearly see. I could have chosen a path of anger, resentment, and regret. That would have been easy to do, believe me. But I knew that wallowing in some low vibrational thought field was just not the best thing for me. This was an opportunity to practice acceptance, to value life's lessons, and to grow into the person I would cherish and respect the most by choosing to move forward in love, peace, and joy. And that's the path I chose.

I want to be clear that, although this was a very difficult life event, I in no way saw myself as a victim. Thankfully, I was able to apply some valuable perspective to the situation and actually felt a deep sense of gratitude and respect for my ex in making a change in her life that she felt was best for her. I knew that, if it was best for her to leave and move on, it was best for me as well. A perspective that I was, and am, deeply grateful for.

Moving forward, I decided to take this great opportunity to just be in my own vibrational energy as much as possible. To spend time with myself and get clear on what I wanted for my life and what I didn't want.

I decided to take full advantage of the spirit of the new year and make some focused resolutions. I promised myself that I would abstain from dating, sex, or otherwise becoming "involved" in any kind of intimate relationship for a period of one year. I felt like that would give me the perfect opportunity to work on myself in a dedicated manner, and to get myself to a place where I would be healed, whole, and the happiest I could be. I chose to clear my home, myself, my energy, and my life of anything and everything that no longer served me or was not in alignment with my Highest-Self. It was one of the wisest choices I've ever made.

"The more I practiced following my own intuition, the easier it became. My intuition and my Higher-Self became my best friends, always there for me, always with my best interest at heart, and always challenging, encouraging, and inspiring me to be the best version of myself."

CHAPTER FIVE

HIGH VIBRATIONAL LIVING

I was excited about this new year, despite the fact that it may have looked like a rocky start. It was a chance for me to "walk the talk" and start living and creating the life I truly wanted for myself. I was filled with a new joy, a sense of personal power, and alignment with my Highest-Self. I decided to actively begin raising my personal vibration higher and higher, which involved, for me, making specific changes in my life and focusing on that as my intention.

One of the first things I did was clear out my house and create a home for myself and my two dogs that felt right for us. I spent a few intense days hauling trash, donating items I knew I would no longer use, and cleaning my house from top to bottom. I know that I function at my best when my environment is not cluttered. I have always preferred a rather sparse living space where I can feel the energy flowing freely and where I can flow freely through the house, unencumbered by a lot of "stuff."

It felt great to repurpose each room in my home to support the lifestyle that I wanted for myself. The main-level office became a small gym complete with free weights and small equipment. The basement where my ex-wife's son lived for many years became my new office. I repainted each bedroom and made the guest bedroom and bathroom very welcoming. One step and one day at a time, I began to simply but effectively make the changes necessary in my home to create the environment that matched what I considered optimal living. This seemed like a very basic concept, but it was, in fact, life changing.

At the same time, I also began to make many repairs around the house, including small things that were not critical or even necessary. This was important to me because I felt strongly that taking good care of what you have is actually gratitude in action. I truly love and cherish my home and consider it an incredible gift. With every small repair, every newly painted room, every cabinet door straightening, and every refrigerator shelf fix, I felt a great sense of my own deep love and gratitude filling every sacred corner of my home. It brought me so much joy to care for something, however temporary a home may be in this life-space, with deep abiding appreciation.

At the time, I had been involved in several local metaphysical groups where the focus was on developing consciousness and raising your vibrations. These groups were wonderful for me, and I decided to actively incorporate some of these simple concepts into my daily life. My good friend, who facilitated the groups and who is a teacher on the evolution of consciousness, Sheila Cash, reminded us of something in one of her weekly teleconferences that stuck with me. Within her words of wisdom, she mentioned that keeping flowers and plants in your environment helps to raise the vibration of the space, and I liked that idea.

My home was shaping up to be the quintessential bachelor pad, heavy on the masculine yang energy. It occurred to me that this was great for my two dogs and myself, but that it might feel a bit unbalanced for any guests. With that in mind, I began the simple act of bringing fresh flowers into the house every week or so and keeping them on the dinning room table. My house is small, so that was the ideal place to keep them where their energy seemed to make the most impact. Grand gestures and changes are nice, but I've always believed the smallest changes can have the biggest impact in our lives. The flowers were so highly vibrational that the feminine yin energy felt like it was enough to balance the whole house.

I also started to change my relationship to my work life. At the time, I had been working in the corporate world for about twenty-six years, and I knew I needed to make some changes in that area as well.

I found an utter lack of integrity in almost every aspect of the industry I was in, which seemed to snowball with each passing year. So much value was placed on beliefs and practices that no longer aligned with my own. Every day that passed, my personal energy felt more and more at odds with the energy of my industry, my job, and the people I dealt with there on a daily basis.

I spent many years operating on the idea of "bloom where you're planted." I did make the best of every situation. I always put my best foot forward. I went about my daily work with great care and dedication. I inserted integrity, generosity, and gratitude into even the smallest of tasks hoping to somehow make a difference, no matter how small or futile my attempts may have seemed. I embraced every opportunity to grow, learn, and expand but I eventually realized I was swimming upstream.

Applying my intent of raising my personal vibration to

all areas of my work seemed daunting. The energy of my work environment simply did not support that. Nevertheless, I began to make those small changes in my work life that I felt would align more with my own Highest-Self. I kept my office clean, uncluttered, and cared for. I remained calm and peaceful while surrounded by the energy of fear and aggression, which was typical and intensifying as the economy plummeted and became increasingly unstable.

I began to take better care of myself by limiting my work hours, disengaging from unrealistic expectations, and putting my own health and wellbeing as a priority over increasing my company's bottom line or perpetuating the false ideas about what success looked like and how to achieve it. It wasn't easy at first, but as my own vibration shifted, I became acutely aware of the magnetic push of non-resonance. Yet, I continued to honor my commitment to keep my vibration on the rise, regardless of the challenges I met along the way.

One of the best shifts I made was in the commitment to acknowledge and honor my own intuition more and more. Even though I've always been aware of my own intuitive nature, somewhere along the line I began to allow the thoughts and feelings of other people to hold more weight than my own, even when I may have had a strong intuitive sense about something. The challenge here for me was that it was often the people whom I loved and respected the most who I allowed to override my own intuitive sense of truth.

Once I finally embraced the idea that what is true for someone else may not always be true for me, I was able to respect other people's truth, void of judgment, while making my own decisions based ultimately on my own knowing and guidance from my Higher-Self. The more I practiced following my own intuition, the easier it became. My intuition and my Higher-Self became my best friends, always there for me, always with my best interest at heart, and always challenging, encouraging, and inspiring me to be the best version of myself. The more I followed my intuition, the more peace and harmony I found in my life.

I've always known that there are actually no answers outside of ourselves and that everything we need, we already have inside us. However, knowing something is not the same as applying it to your life. I spent many years studying, learning, growing, expanding, and essentially "remembering" all of the universal truths we hear about, read about, and go to seminars and workshops to experience from the perspectives of others. It took a conscious choice and deliberate action, though, to systematically activate those truths in my daily living.

It wasn't enough to simply know. I now felt an overwhelming call to take every step possible to live these truths and be a witness to them. I decided to be a living example of universal truth in my own life and boldly forge toward the welcomed, loving, and joyful embrace of self-mastery. What felt risky at first, I soon realized, was just an illusion. In reality, I had nothing to lose that mattered and everything to gain that would ultimately create a life that felt like Heaven on Earth.

Looking at every aspect of my life also meant taking a look at my relationship with money. It seemed the prominent energies around me were somewhat extreme. There were many people in my life who dedicated their lives to increasing their wealth and saving money for retirement so that someday they could be happy. Others focused on winning the lottery. Some were just focused on making ends meet. I was surprised to learn that many were staunchly at odds with the entire money system and had given up on maintaining any kind of working relationship with it. This was one of those challenging situations for me in terms of honoring my own intuitive path. All perspectives were valid, but none seemed to strike the right balance for me.

I had always been pretty responsible, especially with

money. I worked hard, saved, and was discriminating in my spending habits. However, over the past few years, I made some choices that eventually left me with no disposable savings, a good deal of debt, and on a fast financial decline. I had somehow managed to step out of the flow of [1]abundance consciousness and allowed myself to be consumed by the energies around me that were not my own.

Once again, I made some small changes. This time, in my financial life. I prioritized my relationship with money so that it was serving me, rather than the other way around. It did not feel right to me, at the time, to drop out of the monetary system, to whatever extent is actually possible, or to live solely focused on work just to someday have enough to be happy. I made small adjustments that had a huge impact, and I'll share a few of those examples with you.

First, I paid off my debt, which was entirely credit card debt. I used my credit cards to pay for all of my normal expenses and paid them off completely at the end of each month to avoid interest, while gaining a small percent of cash back at the same time. I never paid any fees for using my credit cards, and every so often I would convert my accumulated points to cash. In essence, I was being paid just to use my credit cards. I was very careful to not acquire any further debt. Sure, the banks and merchants were all profiting in the system, but now so was I, and it was good to be back in the flow of [2]abundance energy.

I began investing in myself. Doing away with anything that no longer served my highest good and taking great

---

[1] A conscious awareness which is focused on abundance instead of lack

[2] the vibrational frequency at which abundance is easily attracted/manifested

care of anything that brought me peace and joy. I did small things like my own yard work, cleaning my own home, and as many of my own home repairs as possible. This gave me less time and energy to go out and spend money and more time to move and be active in a healthy and productive way. It also went hand in hand with what I talked about before, in terms of appreciating what I have through active gratitude. None of it seemed like work. I loved it. I had allowed myself to get too busy, and then too busy recovering from being too busy, to enjoy and care for the gifts already around me.

I started to look at other areas of my life where I was choosing to spend money to pay for life's little short cuts. I started to walk or ride my bicycle to run close-by errands. I taught myself how to cook new things and began preparing healthier foods for myself at home rather than eating out. Even though I have always eaten healthfully, it's easier to do so at home because you know what you're eating when you prepare a meal yourself. Restaurant food tends to come with unnecessary and unhealthy amounts of sugar, salt, and other "enhancers." It actually felt great to see my food expenses decrease while my energy levels and vitality increased. It makes sense that a change like this would be good for you, but I gained a new appreciation by doing it myself.

The more changes I made, the more naturally other areas of my life started to change as well. Some longtime friends drifted away, while new friends and acquaintances started to show up. Old groups of friends and community members disbanded, and I found myself drawn to new groups and associations. I had been through cycles like this in my life before, but this time, I was able to appreciate the harmony of the situation as an observer in my own life. Free of attachment to any specific outcome, it became easier and easier to let old energies fall away, and to attract new energies that align with my own intentions for my life.

All of the choices I was now making had a synergistic

impact on my health. I was listening to my own internal guidance, avoiding stress and unreasonable demands, being physically active, eating more consciously, and making joy in the present moment a priority over working toward mainstream ideas of success. I could feel my mind, body, and spirit healing on all levels. I now truly understood the holistic impact of all my decisions and choices in a practical way.

"I began to see that being my true, authentic self in my personal relationships is one of the greatest gifts I can give to someone else. When you are completely you, then you give others the opportunity to love you completely. When you withhold or suppress parts of yourself, it's not possible for someone else to love you completely. We all need someone in our lives to show up for us authentically, to give us the chance to love completely, to have that experience."

CHAPTER SIX

THE AMAZING AUTHENTIC SELF

If I had to choose just one thing to share that I knew would help others create their very best life possible, it would be the powerful choice to discover and be your true authentic self. It seems that the moment we are born, we are taught how to be like everyone else around us. We are shaped and formed by the beliefs, perspectives, habits, and experiences of others. This influences how we relate to ourselves, everyone, and everything we encounter in our lives—every romantic relationship, friendship, job, our family, and so on. Although this is changing more and more as humanity continues to awaken, we are almost never taught what it means to be our true authentic self.

As I took steps to create my best possible life, I became mindful of the fact that it was completely my responsibility to be authentic about what I want. To truly know what you want requires knowing who you truly are. For me, this meant taking a deep personal inventory of every aspect of myself, shedding anything that wasn't actually mine, and bringing to light all that is authentically *me*.

I thought this journey of self discovery might prove to be difficult, but I soon found that it was an endeavor of pure joy. I started with small things, like going to see the kinds of movies I liked, eating the kinds of foods I preferred, surrounding myself with the vibrant colors that energized me, and discarding anything that just wasn't "me." I stopped listening to other people and the constant mainstream media chatter about the next miracle super food, pill, or workout, and I started listening to my own body's feedback on what was best for me and what wasn't. I hung out more with friends and associates who lifted me up and simply avoided people who sapped my energy.

I revisited nearly every belief, pattern, perspective, and habit to examine whether it was true for me. This included some deeply rooted beliefs about myself, life, and others. It included many fears that I absorbed like a sponge over the course of my lifetime but could no longer hold inside me. I was *done* with anything that wasn't my own truth, my own energy, and my own vibration.

Once I began letting go of those parts of my life that no longer served me, I could sense and feel my own vibration growing stronger, which was an amazing experience. I saw the universal Law of Attraction operating with great clarity. I began attracting people, situations, and circumstances into my life that were in harmony with my own vibration. I witnessed stress, disharmony, and dysfunction disappear from my life.

I'm compelled to emphasize just how important it is to do this kind of personal inventory as part of the self-discovery process. Personal authenticity can elude even the most conscious individuals when we're unable to experience ourselves without the constant push-pull of the energies around us. In fact, I had already considered myself to be quite an authentic person well before embarking on this conscious year of change, before I realized my self-image was just an illusion.

With all of these self-imposed changes came natural shifts in the energies around me. I could sense and see the Universe at work, arranging and re-arranging on my behalf. While some doors were closing in my life, others were opening up. It was actually a great relief to me when the circumstances in my life, which I had created by living in-authentically, began to crumble. I could now see that every time I took on something that was not my own, it created another barrier to happiness. Tearing down those barriers created a clear, unobstructed path to my best possible life, and made room for all that is truly and authentically me.

I began to see that being my true, authentic self in my personal relationships is one of the greatest gifts I can give to someone else. When you are completely you, then you give others the opportunity to love you completely. When you withhold or suppress parts of yourself, it's not possible for someone else to love you completely. We all need someone in our lives to show up for us authentically, to give us the chance to love completely, to have that experience. To learn and grow from it. To show up for ourselves that way, and to be that example in the world. This is absolutely necessary to progress on our evolutionary path.

Authenticity is a tool we can use to create our best life

possible. It's a gauge that can let us know when we are aligned with our Highest-Self and when we are misaligned. It provides us the chance to step outside of our situation and be the observer in our own life.

If something isn't going the way we would like, is consuming us or our energy, or is perpetuating disharmony, we can choose to look at where in ourselves we are not being authentic and make a change. We can also see where we have taken on something that is not our own and choose to shed that which is not serving us. Once we consciously practice authenticity, it becomes easier to recognize the changes we need to make to create the life we want.

> "This prayer became one of the most joyful parts of my day. It was perhaps the first time in my life that I truly owned my own faith. I just knew and understood that this was a powerful and loving gift. Perhaps the greatest thing I would ever have to offer anyone."

CHAPTER SEVEN

THE QUANTUM PRAYER

I mentioned earlier that I began to pray for my ex after she left, right at the beginning of the year. I didn't pray for anything specific, just for her best life possible, whatever that would look like for her. I understood the powerful impact of putting high vibrational energy out into the Universe. In fact, I've come to believe that one of the most loving things you can do for another person is to simply and sincerely wish them well. I often put this into practice through active meditative prayer, which ultimately transformed into the work I now call Quantum Prayer.

As I was taking inventory of my life and making a lot of changes, I also began to incorporate Quantum Prayer into other aspects of my life. I defined this earlier as *creating with our intentions through awareness of our infinite nature*. I also mentioned being aware of the experience of being channeled, while also being the channel. I finally understood that I could impact my life and create whatever I wanted through this new awareness.

Within the early weeks of that new year, I began to feel my infinite nature more and more as I became aware that I am the creator of my life now. I always have been, and I always will be. Knowing that relationships are our biggest teachers in this life-space, it occurred to me that there would be many more people coming into my life. I knew I would meet new friends, colleagues, and possibly even find myself in another intimate relationship someday. I knew that those relationships would have their own infinite nature, showing up in past, present, parallel, and future experiences. I also became acutely aware that they would all be happening at once and that whatever I chose to create would manifest in one form or another in each of those experiences.

I asked myself what if I had been more conscious in creating my life much earlier, perhaps even in what we would perceive as the "past"? What would that look like now? What if I choose now to apply Quantum Prayer and create with my intentions through the awareness of my infinite nature? How could I have used that, and how could I use that now, to create the life I want for myself? The answers came to me as fast as the questions, and so I began to put Quantum Prayer into regular practice right away.

It was still early in the new year when I began my regular practice of Quantum Prayer. It was a habit of mine to meditate and pray each night when I went to bed before falling asleep. I decided that, since I may someday find myself in another intimate relationship, it would be amazing to pray for whoever that person might be. Now let me be very clear about something. I did *not* pray for a relationship. I had already decided that I would take the next year to be on my own. I would not entertain being in a relationship of any kind or even casual encounters. In fact, being a middle-aged man (give or take), I knew it was equally possible that I might not be in another intimate relationship in this lifetime. However, now aware of my infinite nature, I did realize that it was likely I would be in some kind of intimate relationship within any one of my life-spaces, including "future" lives.

So I began to simply pray each night for "the woman who is now coming into my life." I didn't get hung up on the wording too much because I knew that this dimension of reality operates more from intent rather than precise wording. I didn't have a specific idea of who this person would be, nor when they might show up, but I wanted to be able to tell her someday that I loved her so much that I was praying for her, for her best life possible, long before we ever met. I wanted to be able to tell her that I thought about her, cared about her, and was thinking of her every day, wishing her well, praying for her to be happy, healthy, and prosperous. Wherever she was, and whatever she was doing, whatever her life was like, I wondered how my loving intentions would impact her. Would she hear me whispering to the Universe on her behalf each night? Would she feel my love radiating into the cells of her body? Would she sense that a deep unconditional love was holding her close? Could she be reaching out to me? What if she was channeling me? Would she recognize me at the core of my being when we ultimately met? Would it, in fact, make any difference?

I began each night with a special Quantum Prayer that I created just for her. Every night, every time I practiced this, the pure love, peace, and joy that I felt grew more and more. I realized, for the first time ever perhaps, that this was *real love*, true, unconditional love. It was the most joyful, loving thing I have ever done in my life. It was not done from any sense of requirement, ceremony, or ritual. It was done each time out of pure enjoyment.

I used the practice of prayer simply because it appealed to me in a basic, straightforward manner. It was the best way for me to be clear about my intentions and to stay in the awareness of my infinite self at the same time. I highly recommend creating your own Quantum Prayers based on your own intentions and in a way that resonates with you. However, this is the special Quantum Prayer I dedicated to "her" every night beginning early in that new year.

The Quantum Prayer

"Dear God, I pray for the woman who is now coming into my life. With all my heart and soul, I reach out to her now to send her my deepest love. I request on her behalf, God, please bless her with enduring optimal health, wellness, and vitality. Where there may be illness, disease, accident, or injury in her life, please restore her and heal her completely. Where there is sadness, grief, or disharmony God, please comfort her and fill her with peace. Where there is fear, anxiety, or anger, please bless her by transmuting those energies into your divine white light. Where there is lack or need in her life, God, please provide and fill her with abundance, wealth, and prosperity. If there is ever a sense of unhappiness, confusion, or distress in her life, God, please always reveal to her the truth of her own divine nature. I ask that you bless her with her very best life possible, God, whatever that would look like for her. Please bless her friends, her family, her work, her environment, and anyone who touches her life in any way. Fill her and surround her with your divine white light and love at all times such that it pours through every cell in her body, every space in between every cell, and radiates through her out into the Universe to bless everyone and everything that she meets. I request all of this in accordance with her own Highest-Self and her own free will. Tell her that I love her, God, that I always have and I always will. When we do meet, in divine right timing, God, I pray that my love resonates with her so deeply, that she recognizes me, and I her. Thank you for the love and the joy of this woman, God. So be it, Amen."

That is essentially the original Quantum Prayer. Although the wording did vary somewhat each time, this is the gist. I would encourage you to stay focused on the intent rather than any specific wording. I can assure you, it was not about using the "correct," exact words, or making sure that I included every possibility and covered every perspective in metaphysical theory. It was simply and purely based on intent, from a place of love and joy, with no attachment to outcome, no judgment about how any of it may or may not manifest or when, all while maintaining the awareness of our divine infinite nature. I was conscious of her every incarnation, every lifetime, albeit past, present, parallel, or future, every unique expression and aspect of her, and so on. This prayer became one of the most joyful parts of my day. It was perhaps the first time in my life that I truly owned my own faith. I just knew and understood that this was a powerful and loving gift. Perhaps the greatest thing I would ever have to offer anyone.

The more I worked with Quantum Prayer, the more it became part of me. I began to feel like I was a "living prayer" and I pretty much remained in a state of persistent awareness and conscious creation. Even though I've always understood the theories about how we receive that which we put out into the world, and what we do comes back to us, and so on, this was a deeper level of understanding conscious creation. Applying it in terms of quantum reality, while understanding our infinite nature, made for exponential possibilities. I had no idea what would actually come of this new reality, or the impact it would ever have on my life. I can tell you for sure, though, that it transformed me, my life, and others around me in ways I could not have predicted.

> "We both recognized a very deep and ancient love between us that neither had ever experienced before. Our connection, our relationship, and our love grew exponentially with every passing day…"

CHAPTER EIGHT

DIVINE CONNECTION

The year of Quantum Prayer was a time of incredible revelation and joy. I dedicated my intentions, went about raising my vibration, shifting my perspective, expanding, growing, learning, and so deeply thankful for all of it.

As that year progressed and was coming to its end, seemingly out of nowhere, I met Susana. It was unexpected and not a conventional meeting by any means. As I said earlier, I was not looking to meet anyone. I did laugh when I realized I had set the intention to give myself a year off from relationships, and it was just about a year later that we met. That was the first of many incredible and revealing synchronicities during that time for us.

While I had spent my entire adult life working in an unrelated industry, I also spent several years simultaneously completing my Doctorate Degree in Naturopathy and had just started my own part-time practice as a Naturopathic Doctor. I had also just completed my certification in a form of healing work called Reconnective Healing® and The Reconnection®. I met Susana because she had completed the same healing certification just about a month prior to me that year, and we actually met on Facebook through that affiliation. I was searching for other practitioners around the world to connect with because of my new practice, and as I was sending out friend requests to anyone associated with this particular work, Susana and I became friends within just a few days of my joining Facebook.

I wasn't into online dating and wasn't interested in any kind of a long-distance relationship. Neither was Susana. However, it was a matter of weeks and a few short months before we began to feel more and more deeply connected. We spent a lot of time getting to know each other, talking, emailing, and sending messages.

Our connection grew so strong, we thought it would be fun to meet each day at the same time and do a meditation together. We lived in different parts of the world, in different countries, and different time zones, so we didn't actually meet in-person at this point. Nevertheless, we agreed to meet in our meditations and then write to each other or meet online and share what we experienced. It was the most amazing and incredible connection I had ever felt in my life. We were both shocked and quickly realized this was no ordinary friendship.

After one of our first meditations together, we were exchanging notes on what we experienced. Although it was very nice, and there were some similarities, it was nothing out of the ordinary really. As we finished sharing, Susana asked me if there was anything else I wanted to tell her about that particular meditation. I said, "Well, not really, but I did put it out there that, if we were really connecting, for you to mention the sun." I picked something that I felt was rather arbitrary. It had been a cold, dreary day, and I was missing the warm days and sunnier weather, so that was just what came to my mind. I wouldn't have mentioned it at all if Susana hadn't asked me that last time if there was anything else. I'm very glad that I did, because Susana went on to tell me about how she had just been outside in a park and sat under a tree writing me a letter about the *sun*, what it meant to her, and how important it was to her. She said she had bought me a pendant of the sun, exactly like the one she wears everyday, and had been carrying it in her pocket for several days and that she was sending me the letter and the sun pendant by mail. Needless to say, I was *overwhelmed* and surprised! It was indeed a synchronicity for us, one of many more to come.

Susana and I both believe that we recognized and "knew" each other almost from the very first meeting online. We both recognized a deep and ancient love between us that neither had ever experienced before. Our connection, our relationship, and our love grew exponentially with every passing day until eventually we did meet in person.

After some time, Susana and I realized who "We" were. We talked, we shared, we allowed ourselves to explore "Us" and it became evident to both of us that we wanted to be together as soon as possible. We experienced a closeness with each other that we tried to find words for, but couldn't. We talked about soul mates, explored twin flames, and anything that seemed to touch on what we were experiencing. We quite literally felt like one soul inhabiting two bodies and that nothing could ever separate us again.

It was during one of our talks that it occurred to me to share with her The Quantum Prayer. I had actually been so overwhelmed with our meeting and all that had transpired, that it was some time before it actually occurred to me that, perhaps, Susana had been the woman for whom I had been praying. I was astounded by my own revelation since I never had an attachment to the outcome of that particular Quantum Prayer.

I started to explain the Prayer to Susana, how it came about, what it was, and that I had realized *she* is the woman in the prayer. I told her that I often wondered if it would ever make a difference, if it would impact her life in a positive way, if she would ever benefit from my well wishes.

It still brings tears to my eyes, no matter how many times I share this part of my story, because it was *the most profound* experience of my life when Susana told me about her past year, that year before we met. Much of this is deeply personal, but I will share with you, in general terms, what Susana shared with me. She said that she did feel a deep longing for a major change in her life, that she felt like there was something else she was meant to do. Something more. She explained that she did experience healing that year. She noticed changes in every aspect of her life including how she related to herself and others. She felt more open and loving to people in general and gained a sincere level of compassionate understanding for the process of life. She experienced healing through her own growth, expanded awareness, and shifts in perspective. She was joyful at a deep interior place of self-love. She said she did feel like my prayers made a difference, and we both agree that perhaps the most significant impact was our own meeting. I was blown away at the realization of it all.

No doubt, Susana and I have a divine connection. Our love, our relationship, is the greatest gift of my life. We often talk about how there really are no words to describe this amazing life we share. It's a treasure that we are profoundly grateful for every moment of each day, never to be taken for granted.

That said, please bear in mind, with healing, growth, and prosperity, also comes change, and that change is not always easy. It is, however, necessary at times. When change comes from a place of love, light, and a knowing that the life you are creating for yourself is based on that same love, light, peace, and joy, the journey of change is one of the most powerful creative processes on which one can embark.

The year Susana and I met was a year of incredible transformation for both of us. I often think that I could never have imagined any of it, but in fact, on some level, I did. I have to believe that Susana imagined our life together as well. Together we co-created a dream, simply by being our own true authentic selves and opening up to allowing the Universe to arrange, re-arrange, and align our vibrational frequencies, all in accordance with our own highest-good.

There is so much more to share about this amazing time in our lives, and I feel compelled to offer that at a later time. Equally compelling is the deeply personal side of Susana's story, which I respectfully defer to Susana to share in her own way, if and when she chooses.

PART THREE

LIVING IN THE NEW CONSCIOUSNES

"...ultimately, we are meant to embody that mastery and walk our path as a living example of that. Mastery was not meant for just a few, like Jesus or Buddha alone, it is meant for everyone."

CHAPTER NINE

OUR NEW REALITY

I've been so blessed to have this opportunity to share my story and this channeled guidance with you. All those years ago, when I first started to work with Quantum Prayer, I had no idea what it all meant, or if it would have meaning to anyone other than myself. However, the more I allowed myself to be open to whatever was meant to be, the more guidance I received and the more I began to understand that there was a distinct purpose.

In this part of the book, I share with you the specific guidance I've received, which describes some of the changes that will take place as humanity and our planet continue to evolve.

Since we have been operating in the dimensions that include linear time, it can be disorienting to experience these shifts, which often seem to operate outside of time. It can also be confusing as we move forward on our evolutionary path to witness aspects of the old consciousness as it transforms and, sometimes, just disappears altogether.

Greater numbers of people are beginning to "wake up" and become more consciously aware, and I know that the Universe has been busy arranging and re-arranging on behalf of humanity to provide a tremendous amount of light on this new path. Often times, these shifts into higher dimensional consciousness can seem like a crumbling, dismantling, or even destruction of aspects of our lives. These aspects have been ingrained in our consciousness and way of living for so long that many people may experience a feeling of being lost, a sense of not knowing what is happening, and may have no idea how to function in the new consciousness.

I sincerely believe that we are all here to actualize our own mastery, which has been an ongoing evolutionary process, for sure. But ultimately, we are meant to embody that mastery and walk our path as a living example. Mastery was not meant for just a few, like Jesus or Buddha alone. It is meant for everyone.

The masters before us brought the higher vibrations of love and light to us and have been holding those vibrations for us, preparing the way. That love and light is meant to reach its full potential in all of us. It's meant to expand and *enlighten.* In fact, *we are* the love and light, and what a beautiful reality to awaken to.

Some of the information I am sharing with you may seem vaguely familiar. That's because there really is no new information. I believe that everything already exists and that we experience it as new when it comes into our conscious awareness. On some level, we "know" that, and we sense that it's more like remembering than learning something for the first time. It's just a matter of awakening to the truth and then consciously operating with a new, enlightened awareness.

The guidance in this book is offered to encourage you on your path, to inspire you to create your own best possible life, to show you what is possible, how to create, manifest, and align with your highest-good. It is my sincere Quantum Prayer that this information, this guidance, this offering, touches your life in a way that neither of us could have foreseen, but that you choose on some level to imagine and create. May it bless your life exponentially, as it has mine.

> "'Cell-f' love requires the awareness of your infinite self and that our intentions can and do manifest on a cellular level. It's the awareness that every cell in our body is a living expression of our intentions. It's based on the dimension of reality where our cells are, in fact, channeling us constantly."

CHAPTER TEN

"CELL-F" LOVE

One of the very first concepts that was shown to me in my channeling work was the concept of "cell-f" love. It was shown to me in this precise way, "cell-f" love, and I understood right away that it was a progression on the major movement in humanity of recent times toward self-love.

Self-love is something that humanity has been working on mastering for some time now. More and more, people have begun to understand just how important self-love is. We've grown to understand that, you can't truly love another person until you learn to love yourself. We've gained the wisdom that the love we have for ourselves is reflected back to us in others. And so on. Learning self-love has been one of the biggest steps in our recent evolution. A significant and critical step, in fact.

Even though many of us are still working on self-love at deeper levels, the consciousness of self-love is at a point where it is ready to expand. This next step into expanded consciousness is "cell-f" love.

"Cell-f" love requires the awareness of your infinite self, and that our intentions can *and do* manifest on a cellular level. It's the awareness that every cell in our bodies are living expressions of our intentions. It's based on the dimension of reality where our cells are, in fact, channeling us constantly. Our cells are persistently communicating with us, speaking to us, and letting us know what they need to flourish. Being aware that our cells want our love and attention is perhaps a small shift in perspective that can have enormous implications in our lives.

"Cell-f" love requires that you consciously connect with the cells of your body and communicate your intentions for their wellbeing, optimal health, and vitality. In a sense, the relationship between us and the cells in our bodies is a microcosm of the macrocosm of divinity. For those of us who practice prayer, we might find ourselves communicating with God, the Universe, our Higher-Self, etc., to consciously co-create something that we want, like good health. It really is the same for the cells in our body. They too are communicating with us as a source of divine love and light to co-create their highest expression as well.

It is fairly typical to go about our daily lives and not give much consideration to our cellular life. After all, our bodies seem to function and operate day in and day out without us giving our cells much thought until something goes wrong. Even then, we haven't really been taught that there is much we can do to affect our cellular life. The truth is, though, that we have simply been unaware. We can create health and wellbeing for our cellular life simply and effectively.

One of the easiest ways to create cellular health and vitality is to actively communicate with our cells. As I was channeling this particular guidance, I was taken into a deep meditative state where I would bring my cells into my conscious awareness. I could sense my cells interdimensionally, meaning I was aware of my cells in every incarnation, in every lifetime, in every form, aspect, and expression for which I exist now, have existed, and will ever exist, and as part of my true infinite nature. While staying connected at this cellular level, I simply expressed my deepest gratitude, love, and appreciation for every cell. As I did this, I could see my cells, in every form, respond by becoming brighter and brighter, emanating and reflecting love back to me and all through my body. I continued to send my cells, each one, divine love and light. I aligned my intentions with creating healthy, vibrant, loving, joyful cells. As I did so, I could feel love, light, joy, and peace flood my body and every body that has ever been a part of me. It was in this deep meditative state that I first experienced the powerful, creative force of "cell-f" love.

It was amazing to me to be introduced to such a simple but profound way of relating to my body. I thought how wonderful it would be to just meditate and send love and light to all of my cells all the time! It felt incredible, and I wanted to stay in that place, expressing and communicating love and light. I instinctively knew the healing and transformative effect this would have, and I wanted to find a way to maintain it.

I quickly realized that this was just another form of Quantum Prayer, but focused at the cellular level. Now that "cell-f" love had been brought into my consciousness, it would remain accessible through just my awareness. I could essentially remain in that state of conscious awareness and demonstrate a continuous *living prayer*, on behalf of my cells and co-create the healthiest, most vibrant, and joyful cellular life possible.

I will say that it is easy to go about my daily life and fall into an unconscious state and become disconnected from my cells. But, it's not as easy as it was before, and I am staying in that state of constant connection and awareness much more. That's the key. To become more and more aware and continually return to the higher dimensional realities where creating cellular health is the norm rather than out of reach.

I encourage you to incorporate "cell-f" love into your day. A meditation like the one I described worked well for me, but there are many other ways to make the connection. As I was channeling this guidance, I was shown many possibilities. They include options like singing to your cells, drawing pictures of your cells using healthy, vibrant colors, and something that I could only describe as "cellular massage" where you just envision touching every cell in your body with gentle love and tenderness.

At some point, "cell-f" love will be so ingrained in our consciousness that it will be as much of our normal understanding as the concept of self-love is now. We won't have to think about it; we will live it and be examples of it. Our bodies will express it through our cellular co-creation. In essence, our cellular expression will exude the love that we give to our cells. It can be used for healing, of course, but it will also evolve to a point where healing is no longer required, because we will have mastered "cell-f" love and will be choosing to only create healthy cells and a healthy cellular life.

"Many of my clients have shared their own stories of how they 'woke up' and realized they no longer could sustain themselves in the energies of old consciousness—of lack, fear, constant competition, and valuing money and the hope of someday retiring and being happy—over being happy and healthy right now."

CHAPTER ELEVEN

COOPERATION

Although the idea of cooperation is not new, it is evolving in our consciousness to take on a new kind of energy. As we continue to shift into the higher dimensional realities, cooperation significantly overtakes the lower vibrational energy of competition. I'm talking about the kind of competition that fosters the consciousness of "lack" and "not enough." The kind of competition that perpetuates the idea that, if someone else wins or gains something, then someone else has to lose.

This is such a crucial shift in our awareness, because it has a huge impact on our energetic vitality. A majority of humanity has operated primarily within a state of constant competition. We go to school as children and compete against each other through a grading system, and then for access to higher education. We go out into the business world and compete for jobs. Within those jobs, we compete with our colleagues and other businesses to gain as much income, notoriety, and "security" for ourselves as possible. We actually spend our lives in this competitive mode, believing that resources are finite and that, if someone else prospers, it's at our expense. This lifelong consciousness is one of the biggest energy drains on our planet. It creates enormous amounts of stress in our daily lives, it fosters war among nations and people, and it perpetuates choices based on fear rather than love.

It's been a long-held belief that competition is healthy and that it is necessary to motivate people to strive for a better life, to produce higher levels of quality services and products, and to continue to gain more of whatever it is we want for ourselves. In fact, the theory of our own evolution is based on competition and survival of the fittest.

Competition has been a great teacher for us. It's been a tool and a benchmark we've used to learn and grow, similar to linear time. However, in the higher dimensional realities, competition in its current form just isn't necessary. In fact, it can't exist. Once we evolve to a certain level of understanding, the consciousness required to sustain competition is superseded by the new consciousness of our infinite nature. Once we are aware of our infinite nature, that we have always existed and that we always will, we no longer operate from a place of fear, lack, and extinction.

Being free from the fear of lack, we naturally shift our energy from a competitive state to a state of cooperation, and we gain more than we ever could have realized in the old energies. The new consciousness of cooperation works on basic universal laws, such as the Law of Reciprocity, which essentially means that what we send out into the Universe comes back to us. We learn a new way of creating: through cooperation rather than competition. Cooperation then becomes a natural expression of the Universal Laws of Reciprocity, Attraction, and so on.

In the evolution of humanity, we are already beginning to see the shift toward cooperation. There are food coops, housing coops, and even educational coops. Even some government entities are demonstrating cooperation by planting food gardens in public parks for public sharing and consumption. There are some people who are operating completely outside the current monetary system, and they support themselves by an exchange of services and energy rather than money. Granted, these people are few in number, but they are masterfully creating and holding the vibration of cooperation for our planet. These higher vibrational energies are exponentially more powerful than the old vibrational energies of competition. Therefore, it takes fewer people holding this vibration for it to grow and overcome the old consciousness.

I meet more people everyday who have simply chosen to drop out of the corporate consciousness that fosters competition at its highest levels. Many of my clients have shared their own stories of how they "woke up" and realized they no longer could sustain themselves in the energies of old consciousness—of lack, fear, constant competition, and valuing money and the hope of someday retiring and being happy—over being happy and healthy right now.

We will see cooperation in its many forms taking over where competition has left us exhausted, fearful, and diseased. The amount of energy we regain is immeasurable. The more we function in the consciousness of cooperation, the more we will prosper in every area of life. The stress and anxiety that create illness and disease will begin to fade, giving way to peace and vitality. Our value system will shift to align with the consciousness of love, peace, and joy as a basic economy.

"The foundation for my own naturopathic and healing practice has been that even the smallest shift in perspective can bring about the greatest healing."

CHAPTER TWELVE

SHIFTING PERSPECTIVE TO HEAL

I've noticed a trend over the course of my adult life, where there seems to be more illness and disease that baffles conventional medicine. These show up as ailments and chronic illnesses that are either treated on the surface through symptom management or dismissed entirely as nothing to be concerned about. Sometimes, conventional medicine will outright admit that a cause of illness or a plan for healing is just not within its grasp.

We often find ourselves looking to alternative or complimentary philosophies to help us understand the root causes of illness and how to heal. For quite some time, many spiritual teachers and metaphysicians have been educating us about disease, illness, the root causes, as well as the spiritual and energetic components of illness.

We've come to understand certain philosophies, such

as the idea that we are energetic beings, that illness is created to teach us a lesson, and that illness occurs when there is some sort of imbalance in ourselves and/or our lives. All of these are true, and so we've trended increasingly toward energy forms of healing, alternative and naturopathic approaches, and any number of modalities that recognize the need for balance and the role of energy, thought forms, emotions, and beliefs in our overall health and wellbeing.

Many master teachers have served humanity by bringing to light new perspectives on illness and ways to heal from it. They have taught us so much about what illness is, what true healing means, and how neither is a force outside of ourselves. These teachers and healers have held the frequency of vibrational healing and understanding for our planet and have paved the way for the next generation of healing through shifts in our perspective.

The foundation for my own naturopathic and healing practice has been that even the smallest shift in perspective can bring about the greatest healing. This has been demonstrated in my personal life and healing journeys numerous times. Each time I would encounter some sort challenge, I realized that it was my perspective that would slow down, or even block, my desired progress toward healing.

So what is it about shifting perspective that can result in healing for us? First, the very idea that healing *can* occur is an important step. We've been trained by mass media and the conventional medical culture to believe that we need "this pill" or "that procedure" in order to improve our health and wellbeing. On top of that, many laws and healthcare programs dictate that we follow the prescriptive model of healthcare while limiting any other approach to healing. There is also a prevalent fear factor that we often encounter when we try to step outside of conventional medicine. We are faced with the long-held beliefs that only conventional medicine can heal; anything else is unsafe or risky.

It is the small shifts in perspective that propel us forward toward healing. Some of these shifts might include things like recognizing stress in our life, understanding the impact of our thoughts and emotions on our health, accepting total responsibility for our own wellbeing, and so on. These are some of the ideas and concepts that we've been incorporating into our conscious awareness and have made great strides in affecting healing in our lives because of them.

As we continue to evolve in consciousness and we operate more in the higher dimensional realities, we will find that these small shifts in perspective take on a quantum aspect that promotes the possibility of total, and even instant, healing. In being consciously aware of our infinite nature, we can apply these shifts to every incarnation and every unique expression of ourselves and essentially eradicate all illness and disease we've accumulated through our life experiences.

One practical example I like to use is the perpetually hot topic of diet and nutrition. Somewhere along the way we accepted the idea that we are all the same and should all eat in a specific way to be healthy. So much has been misunderstood about diet and nutrition, and these long-held beliefs have created chronic illness. In my own practice, I use a [ii]Unique Nutritional Profile™ to demonstrate how each of us is unique in our nutritional requirements and how we can use that shift in perspective to maximize our health and vitality. Once we shift our perspective on nutrition from that of the mass consciousness and become aware of our unique nutritional needs, our bodies can often respond immediately. In reality, that one small shift in perspective can effectively change your entire life as well as those around you, *forever*.

The potential for small perspective shifts are infinite in themselves. Any number of shifts can produce tremendous healing when we incorporate them into our conscious awareness. One of those shifts is a concept that I touched on earlier—when I let go of the idea that I had to wait to be happy.

I was brought up in the consciousness, as many of us are, that you go to school, get a job, work, work, work, save for retirement, and after you've sacrificed and waited long enough, then you can rest, take care of yourself, and be happy. Nowadays we are beginning to realize the risk in that particular model of existence.

I've seen many people work their entire lives and lose their retirement benefits before getting to use them. Many people subject themselves to so much wear and tear over their lifetime, once they reach retirement, if they are lucky enough to do so, they aren't well enough to enjoy it. Gambling on whether happiness is waiting for you somewhere down the road is risky; although, we've allowed ourselves to believe that it is the only safe choice to make.

My shift in perspective about this allowed me to open my consciousness to an expanded awareness that included infinite possibilities for happiness *now* rather than some point in the future. With this new awareness, I was able to see that I had choices I could make that would allow me to create the life I wanted, and so, I did just that.

Having let go of, quite literally, a lifetime of limited consciousness, all of the associated fear, stress, and anxiety simply melted away. Once that happened, tremendous healing occurred in my body, mind, spirit, and really, in every aspect of my life. It was a *quantum* shift.

Another shift occurred for me several years ago when I experienced the sudden onset of one of the most painful and scary health issues of my life. I had somehow contracted what is thought to be a rare virus, which embedded in the nerve bundles in my shoulders, damaging the nerves so severely in both shoulders that I lost use of both arms from my shoulder to my elbow. Since the nerves were damaged, the muscles served by those nerves wasted away rapidly within a few days. Essentially, my arms hung from my shoulders nearly useless.

I was very sick at the time and actually ended up in the hospital where they ran every conceivable test on me for days trying to figure out what happened. As I was discharged, I was told they didn't exactly know what happened and that there wasn't much of anything they could do to help me. They prescribed physical and occupational therapy and said that, although it was possible to regain some nerve function in the distant future, I should start learning how to live with my disability.

Confused by the experience, I dutifully started physical therapy right away. I ended up in a room full of other people in rehabilitation where each therapist was working with several patients at once. Mine would stick me on a machine, instruct me on what to do for the next ten minutes, then rotate to another patient. It didn't take long for me to realize this was a slow, expensive road to nowhere.

I was acutely aware of every cell in my body channeling me with a resounding urgency to respectfully decline the prognosis and the prescriptive course of therapy. I sensed in every ounce of my being that I could and would heal quickly, and that I would instinctively know how to manifest that for myself.

I shifted my perspective from the conventional medical model belief system to believing in myself. It is wise and often beneficial to take in the experience and opinions of professionals, especially when it comes to matters of our health and wellbeing, but I will never again dismiss the wisdom of my own body and spirit in favor of anyone else's. There are no answers outside of ourselves and no one knows our bodies better than we do. Sometimes our bodies may agree with the conventional medical model, but when it doesn't, making that small shift in perspective can make all the difference in the world.

I truly believed this experience with my arms was temporary and that I would heal quickly. I actually *knew* it would make me stronger in the long run. I began doing full-body workouts with a personal trainer several times a week and started to see rapid improvements right away.

There were a few significant keys to my healing that I knew would make all the difference in the world for me. I was working with a trainer whose mindset was on building muscle and physical fitness. He could not have cared less what shape I was in when I got to him. He worked with many people at all levels of physical fitness and knew the formula for powerful transformation. He never saw me as sick or disabled. Being in that energy was exactly what I needed. It left no room for anything other than improvement, and he fully expected to see me getting stronger every day. I believed it, too, and that is exactly what happened.

It was a matter of a few months before I had regained full use of both my shoulders and arms and saw that I would be even stronger than before. Lesson learned. I will never trust anyone more than I trust myself.

We are evolving to a point in consciousness where we will inventory our perspective to reveal causes of some of our most prevalent chronic conditions. We will experience the phenomenon of instant, spontaneous, and permanent healing when these shifts occur. Once you experience one of these small shifts, whatever it may be for you, healing in this manner of awareness will become instinctual.

Many of the topics and ideas discussed here with you may elicit a shift in perspective. Perhaps many shifts. As each area of guidance comes into your conscious awareness, infinite opportunities arise for healing. However, the choice to heal remains subject to your own free will, as always.

> "...forgiveness is only required for healing until we step out of duality and victim consciousness and become aware that there was nothing to forgive in the first place. So, in effect, forgiveness is not required for healing, nor does it exist, in the higher dimensional realities."

CHAPTER THIRTEEN
CREATIVE EVOLUTION

One of the most liberating differences we will find in the new consciousness is the absence of victim consciousness. Victim consciousness keeps us in a low state of energy, because functioning at this level of consciousness requires us to give our power to others.

When we experience ourselves as victims, we take on the perspective that everything is happening to us and that we have no control over our circumstances or our lives. We often blame others and shift responsibility away from ourselves. It may seem like we gain energy this way, because it relieves us of responsibility. That is an illusion, and actually the opposite is true. It will always take less energy to take full responsibility for ourselves than it will trying to be happy while others are responsible for us.

When we perceive others as being responsible for our happiness and wellbeing, we give away our power and lose energy.

Another aspect of old consciousness that is dissolving is duality consciousness. For the purposes of this discussion, duality is the idea that something has to be one or the other (good or bad, young or old, masculine or feminine). Duality suggests a separateness of aspects rather than a unification. Duality also lends itself to judgment, which can also feed the old victim consciousness.

As an example, lets say a man leaves his wife for another woman. The wife may feel like the victim. Like her husband betrayed her and is the cause of her pain. She may also look at the situation as bad, and that marrying him in the first place was a bad idea. She begins to judge him, herself, the situation, and every other related aspect, such as mutual friends, the other woman, any children they had together, the home they shared, and so on. All the while, she feels helpless to do anything to improve her happiness.

In duality and victim consciousness, we remain stuck by giving our energy and power to another person, based on the illusion that the current situation is either bad or good at any given moment, and is completely the responsibility of someone other than ourselves.

When we align with the higher dimensional realities where creative evolution is understood, duality and victim consciousness cannot and do not exist. With creative evolution, we have the distinct awareness of our infinite selves. We understand that we are souls that have chosen every aspect of our lives, every circumstance, and every event for the singular purpose of learning the lessons our soul has chosen to learn in order to evolve.

With every incarnation, souls do collectively agree to help one another in this respect. For example, if two souls are choosing to learn forgiveness, one may agree to be the betrayer and the other the betrayed, thereby creating the circumstances for which forgiveness can be used in healing. Both souls are simply playing a roll for each other to learn, grow, and evolve. In this light, there is no victim, and there really is no right or wrong. Two souls simply had an agreement and actually co-created the circumstances with which the agreement would be fulfilled.

In the example of the husband leaving his wife, she could become consciously aware of her own creative evolutionary process. She would see her husband leaving as neither good nor bad. She would not judge the other woman for her role in the co-creation. She would not perceive the resulting circumstances as being out of her control. She would simply incorporate the lesson into her consciousness and leave behind what no longer serves her.

In this same example, the wife never really loses energy or gives up her own power. She is able to accept the lesson and the situation as a gift and begin to use her own energy to move forward in her evolutionary process having gained the perspective. Once she is operating more in this higher dimensional reality, she can begin to see how to use this reality to create the life she would want for herself.

It is possible to learn our life lessons through love, peace, and joy rather than illness, pain, and disappointment. Once we are aware that we are creating the circumstances in our life, we can then make the choices that reflect our best life possible. Granted, this is something that can take time to master while still waffling between dimensional realities. For others, it can take the form of a quantum shift. Either way, once that shift occurs, and you stay in the awareness of your infinite self, conscious evolution can be applied to every aspect, expression, and incarnation of yourself affecting a radical healing at every level of your existence.

It's also important to note that the concept of forgiveness is associated with the old victim and duality consciousness. We've spent a great deal of time and energy in our recent life-spaces learning that we must learn to forgive ourselves and others for healing to take place. This is absolutely true within the context of old consciousness. However, forgiveness is only required for healing until we step out of duality and victim consciousness and become aware that there was nothing to forgive in the first place. So, in effect, forgiveness is not required for healing, nor does it exist, in the higher dimensional realities.

Another way that creative evolution is expressed is through our DNA. It is common to think of our DNA as something that we are born with and stuck with, in terms of our genetic expression. In other words, we experience ourselves as being limited by our DNA. Some examples of those limiting beliefs might include things like being able to gain or lose weight, genetic health conditions, male pattern baldness, longevity, and so on.

Particularly as we approach a certain age, we are invited into the illusion that we will manifest the same diseases of our parents and grandparents. You will be delighted to know that you can choose to decline that invitation. In fact, our DNA is actually accessible to us, ever-evolving, and changeable.

In the higher dimensional realities, our DNA is experienced more as an expression of our consciousness. My understanding is that the ways in which we can affect our DNA expression is as limitless as our own infinite nature. We only need to be aware of our infinite nature while consciously creating the DNA expression that we choose.

The best way that I can convey this reality to you is to share exactly what I was shown in the course of my channeling work.

I was shown, as discussed earlier in the Introduction, the original seed of light that is essentially who we really are. At our core, we are this pure, divine, love and light. From that seed of light, I was shown every incarnation, lifetime, aspect, and unique expression, as well as every evolutionary path for each. I saw how our DNA expression evolved with each of those paths based on our various decisions and intentions. I was also shown that we could, in our infinite awareness, essentially change the present expression of our DNA by clearing from our DNA anything that no longer serves us and retaining that which is in alignment with our Highest-Self.

I'll walk you through this specific process a little later in the book. For now, it's important to know that, once we are aligned with our Highest-Self, our decisions and intentions may be very different than what we originally thought. For example, if our soul chose to come into this particular life-space with a specific disability, or distinct physical difference from what we might consider "the norm," to learn a lesson or as part of an agreement to help another soul learn a lesson, then that may be something that our High-Self would not choose to change. From that level of consciousness, the disability or distinct difference is neither good nor bad, it simply exists to accomplish the intended goal. So once we are operating in these higher dimensional realities where we can make such changes, it doesn't necessarily mean we would choose to do so.

"The energy of a divine marriage is so distinct, there will be no doubt when you find yourself within its grace."

CHAPTER FOURTEEN

THE NEW FAMILY SYSTEM

Our family system has certainly been changing in recent history, but still fundamentally looks and functions the same as it has for thousands of years. It's not quite as rigid as it once was, though. In addition to the typical family structure of one man and one woman coming together, having children, and repeating that pattern from generation to generation, we now have many more variations on what we consider family.

Family is now defined more on an individual basis and looks and functions differently for each of us. Forming a family and creating a family life is no longer limited by factors such as gender, how children are brought into the family, the status of extended family members, and so on.

Even the purpose of forming a family has shifted from the basic model of survival, mutual support, and raising children to include any number of more personal factors. Since relationships are one of our greatest teachers, and families are a significant product of relationships, it stands to reason that families then form the dynamic structure for some of our greatest life lessons.

The aspect of learning from relationships and family dynamics will remain with us even in higher dimensional realities. However, our consciousness about relationships and families will be new. We are beginning an era when duality is fading away and we understand ourselves and our relationships in a new light. We are beginning to experience a kind of spiritual interdependence rather than a survival dependence. We are forming what author and spiritual teacher, Gary Zukav, describes as [iii]spiritual partnerships, which are relationships between partners who come together for the purpose of spiritual growth.

As we deepen our understanding of our own infinite nature, it becomes easier to apply the same awareness to other people. Since victim and duality consciousness do not exist in the higher dimensional realities, neither does judgment. In the absence of judgment, we have a clearer path to learning and development. In a sense, we have less muck to wade through so we are able to move through our growth process quickly. That is one of the reasons humanity and our planet are now evolving at a more rapid pace.

A common trend we will begin to see more of relates to marriage. Marriage has mostly been instituted by government and religion to this point. There are some people who have functioned in a marriage-like union outside of those entities, but civil and religious marriage has been the standard. Along with the institution of marriage came many laws, regulations, responsibilities, and so on. These were seen as necessary, given that the dominant purpose in forming a marriage was to ensure survival, provide mutual support, and rear children.

The new marriages, which are based on spiritual partnership, will not need the former structure of civil and religious regulation. These marriages will be formed and operate from the higher dimensional realities and will not be subject to the heavier energies of duality, victim consciousness, or judgment.

Each partner will operate as an equal contributor to the marriage and family. It will be clearly understood that the relationship carries the divine intent of spiritual growth and all dynamics, challenges, issues, and life events will be processed through this lens of clarity. Because of this high vibrational agreement, we are sure to see fewer divorces and broken families.

This is not to say that a spiritual partnership can't exist within the sanctified parameters of civil or religious marriage. They can, and many will. In fact, people who may have been disillusioned by previous marriages could find themselves completely detached from the old consciousness of marriage and thoroughly compatible with the new. The energy of a divine marriage is so distinct, there will be no doubt when you find yourself within its grace. The old concerns simply will not apply.

These new spiritual partnerships will have an obvious impact on all associated relationships, children, and extended family. This incredible shift in purpose will be the solid foundation for the new family system and a major step in our planetary evolution toward Heaven on Earth.

> "On an individual level, this will result in increased personal energy, a rapid reduction of stress, illness, and disease, as well as an overall sense of peace and joy. For many it will reveal a deep level of personal purpose and fulfillment…"

CHAPTER FIFTEEN

BEING VS. STRIVING

Living in the new consciousness of higher dimensional realities will provide us with opportunities to experience life through a state of *being* rather than *striving*.

Striving can feel like swimming upstream, going against the current, or trying to fit a square peg into a round hole. No matter how much we strive, we seem to be working against a force greater than ourselves. The truth is, though, that we are not. When we strive relentlessly only to meet persistent resistance, that force, which seems outside of us, is actually a reflection of our Higher-Self within requiring balance.

I'm not speaking of the kind of striving in which we set a goal and work steadily to achieve it. I'm speaking of the kind of striving that suggests a struggle or fight. The kind of striving in which we keep doing the same things over and over again, expecting different results, and depleting our energy while doing so. This kind of striving actually indicates that we are operating out of alignment with our Higher-Self.

I've had several periods in my own life when I've found myself striving relentlessly for one thing or another. Whether it was a promotion at work, peace in a relationship, or a specific physical or emotional healing, my energy would eventually get so depleted that my daily life was quite miserable.

With energy reserves so low, it's easy to start to try to replace them artificially. This might result in anything from consuming an excess of caffeine, sugar, or food in general to throwing ourselves entirely into our work at the exclusion of all else, or pursuing one unhealthy relationship after another to fulfill our need for connection. Striving almost always leads to greater imbalance as we seek to compensate for the loss of energy. These imbalances then begin to manifest as illness, disease, poor relationships, unhappiness or even depression.

Fortunately, humanity is awakening to the higher dimensional realities, which exemplify universal truths such as the Law of Least Effort. This doesn't mean going through life without ever making an effort. It simply demonstrates the principles of harmony and that when we come to a place of acceptance and non-resistance, we find ourselves naturally in the flow of conscious creation where all things are possible. It's a fantastic barometer that tells us when we are meeting resistance, that there is another, more balanced way to achieve our objective gracefully and in alignment with our higher-Self. When we are tuned into this higher dimensional reality, we are in a state of being rather than striving.

So what will this look like for us in this new era of higher consciousness? We will begin to see major shifts around us and on our planet. People are seeking balance like never before. Many people will switch to jobs that are more in harmony with their Higher-Selves. As this happens, there will be huge shifts in employment and in our economy. We may experience a wave of people leaving the traditional workforce, as well as a restructuring of corporations and governments.

The result of these shifts on a planetary level will be higher quality productivity with less energy required and greater benefits. This will result in a shift of values where compensation is commensurate with harmony and most people will be thriving in their field rather than striving.

On an individual level, this will result in increased personal energy, a rapid reduction of stress, illness, and disease, as well as an overall sense of peace and joy. For many, it will reveal a deep level of personal purpose and fulfillment previously inaccessible in the lower dimensional realities.

We will also see a shift in relationships where many will choose to respectfully leave situations that are not in harmony with their Higher-Self and naturally align with partners and family members who co-create love, peace, and joy through balance, non-judgment, and acceptance.

This incredible state of being will infiltrate humanity, leading to the greatest levels of personal and planetary peace and fulfillment that we have ever experienced. This is yet another example of how our life in the new consciousness will create Heaven on Earth.

> "Since we are mirrors for other people as well, we can assume that anytime someone is judging us, we are serving to reflect back to them something about themselves that needs to be revealed for their own healing and growth."

CHAPTER SIXTEEN

REFLECTIONS IN THE MIRROR

Humanity is now experiencing a rapid transformation in how we see ourselves in relationship to others by stepping out of the illusion of duality. It's been fairly common to use other people as a sort of benchmark against our own self-image to determine how well we are doing. When we begin to operate more in the higher dimensional realities where duality and separateness do not exist, we no longer perceive other people, or aspects of other people, as outside of ourselves.

A shift in perspective allows us to experience aspects of ourselves in everyone we meet. We are all, in fact, mirrors for each other. Instead of perceiving the people we judge as separate from ourselves, we can now choose to see those people, or aspects of them, as a reflection of some part of us. The other person serves as a mirror, revealing to us our own nature as a way to help us learn, grow, and evolve.

The Universal Law of Attraction demonstrates that we always attract people, situations, and circumstances into our lives that are vibrating at our own frequency. So we are, in essence, always attracting that which is similar to us.

Intimate relationships are the perfect example of this phenomenon. So much energy is expended and angst is created when we exercise judgment in our personal relationships. For example, we may begin to see some characteristic in our partner that we perceive as dismissive or rude. We may notice how he or she relates to other people and assign judgment to that particular behavior or attitude. At that point, we have two options.

Option one is fairly common in the old consciousness. We can perceive our partner as rude and unfriendly and become disturbed. That disturbance may cause us to feel uncomfortable with our partner, especially in public or social situations. We may choose to point out to our partner that we find them rude or unfriendly when they demonstrate certain behaviors. We may even become dissatisfied with our partner and start to withdraw from them when those situations arise. This often leads to a viscous cycle of judgment, which can serve energetically to co-create disharmony.

The second option is more common in the higher dimensional realities where we do not experience ourselves as separate from one another. We may observe the same behavior and perceive it as rude or unfriendly and instead of judging our partner, we immediately recognize the situation as a reflection of how we actually perceive ourselves. In other words, we see in our partner that which is inside of us. We understand that our partner is in service to us, revealing those parts of us that we need to become aware of and heal. In this case, we would look at ourselves and where and how we are demonstrating rudeness or unfriendliness in our own life.

Once we accept this level of consciousness into our

awareness, we gain back the energy that has been expended judging others and ourselves. We drop judgment altogether in favor of self-reflection, growth, and healing.

Since we are mirrors for other people as well, we can assume that anytime someone is judging us, we are serving to reflect back to them something about themselves that needs to be revealed for their own healing and growth. In the old consciousness, we may have allowed ourselves to feel criticized when this happens. We may even go so far as to struggle by questioning ourselves, as if something is wrong with us. In the new consciousness we can recognize such judgment for what it is and not take it personally. This frees up an enormous amount of personal energy.

It's a tremendous leap in consciousness when we can begin, not just to perceive, but also *experience* ourselves as not being separate from one another. We realize that any struggle anyone has ever faced is a struggle we have also faced at some point in our infinite existence.

Ultimately, we learn, heal, and grow exponentially when we choose to experience life as a reflection of our own nature. The more we do this, the faster we heal and evolve. As we do so, we begin to see that growth, that which is healed within us, reflected back to us in love, peace, and joy. As we heal and grow, so does everyone and everything around us.

> "When we experience learning in its true form of remembering, it's no longer necessary to learn through memorization in the way that we have been accustomed."

CHAPTER SEVENTEEN
LEARNING THROUGH CONSCIOUS AWARENESS

One of the most significant transitions we will experience in the higher dimensional realities is the shift from learning mostly through study and memorization, to learning through our conscious awareness. That doesn't mean the current model of education will become obsolete anytime soon, but we will find that by virtue of simply being more conscious we are naturally more inclined toward a deeper level of awareness.

There are several factors that will influence how we learn and grow in the new consciousness. The most prominent factor being our increasing ability to tap into the grid of universal consciousness. Since everything has always existed, all knowledge and wisdom has also always existed and is available in consciousness. The more we operate in the higher dimensional realms where quantum reality prevails, the more aware we are of that availability of accessing information.

With the awareness of our infinite nature, we also begin

to understand that we have access in the present moment to all that exists. We've chosen to operate behind a kind of veil for the purpose of our soul evolution, but that does not mean it doesn't exist or that it isn't available to us. When we experience learning in its true form of remembering, it's no longer necessary to learn through memorization in the way that we have been accustomed.

There are many souls on our planet who have been masterfully holding the vibration of this reality for us. They often are those we perceive under the labels of autistic and savants. These incredible beings can display levels of mathematical or musical genius seemingly beyond our grasp. They operate so much in the higher dimensional realities, it can often be difficult, if not impossible, for them to integrate fully into current society. They have served humanity in a role we are only beginning to appreciate.

Another factor in learning through conscious awareness is an increasing cooperation with our own intuition. As we grow to value and incorporate the wisdom of our intuitive nature, we will less often look outside ourselves for answers. That's because our true essence is not of separateness, but of oneness and completeness. Our intuition can be thought of then as the collective consciousness that resides within us. Any particular life-space can be thought of as an expression of the collective consciousness, *born from all that is*, rather than separate from all that is.

So in practical terms, what will this new learning through conscious awareness look like? We will begin to see several shifts in our educational system that will support the role of consciousness in learning. We will be guided to a more cooperative role with our own intuition and be encouraged to experience ourselves through our own infinite nature.

In the portion of our life experience still operating in linear time, this shift will take the form of expanded awareness in our classrooms and at a much earlier point in our lives. Our school systems will begin to include programs for expanding conscious awareness and will start to function outside of former constraints such as rigid routine and the illusion of separateness. All of these changes are the natural progression of our planetary evolution and will soon overtake our current conventional educational system.

I will also share with you what I have been shown as a possible model for continued growth as we operate more in the higher dimensional realities. It seems that rapid evolution will propel us to a form of gathering together to share our collective consciousness rather than assembling within the structure of traditional classrooms.

We will learn, grow, and evolve in a more experiential context than we ever have before. Tests won't be handed out and graded by teachers necessarily, but conducted within the context of experience. Although this is similar to the kind of learning we currently encounter on an emotional level, it will apply just as well to every level at which we experience ourselves.

Along with this shift to higher dimensional learning is a balance that takes place in valuing our teachers and guides. Teachers, who play one of the most crucial roles in our society, have been so undervalued that it has exponentially slowed down our progress. That is beginning to change, and we will start to see the true value of our teachers compensated on a more universally conscious scale.

Another trend in learning through conscious awareness has to do with the role of art in our evolutionary process. Artists have a special role in tapping into the collective consciousness, which means that the messages conveyed through their art have the potential to reach humanity en masse. When artists choose to use this platform to raise consciousness, the evolutionary process of humanity and our planet is accelerated exponentially.

Although we've already experienced a great deal of

learning through this form of consciousness, we will most definitely begin to see a big shift in art toward the higher dimensional realities. Artists will engage in consciously creating their media to convey everything from new ways of healing, mathematics, engineering, human relations, and so on. There really is no limit to the subject matter when it's conveyed through the creative force of art.

I also think of artists as being a kind of channel. They serve humanity by producing the media in its various forms, such as movies, music, poetry, painting, books, etc., which hold the frequency of light required for our learning, growth, expansion, and evolution. We will begin to see Art modeling for humanity what it looks like to live and operate in the higher dimensional realities, bringing an increasing amount of light to our planet. It is the exquisite way we learn through an expanded awareness.

PART FOUR

CONCLUSION

"Of course we will still use conscious language, but the focus will shift from using the exact metaphysically perfect words in every case, to radiating our pure intentions to the Universe through authenticity and deep awareness."

CHAPTER EIGHTEEN

LANGUAGE AND INTENTION

Many spiritual teachers have devoted a great deal of time and energy bringing the concept of conscious language to humanity. This has been one of the most significant concepts in helping us understand how our words and thoughts affect every part of our lives.

For me, the general idea of choosing and using words that are in alignment with what I want to create for myself makes good sense. Words have an energy signature about them and are an incredibly powerful tool for creating.

The reason language has such a powerful impact on what we create is because of the level of consciousness embedded in the words we have used to communicate with each other for such a long period of time. We've been taught that certain words imply specific intent. In that way, we can all understand each other due to the fact that the words we are taught already hold an intent and carry that energy signature. This has worked remarkably well, of course.

Using language with conscious awareness will always be an important part of creating our lives. However, I've been shown that we have hit critical mass in understanding the importance of language and that this universal tool for creation is now ingrained enough into mass consciousness, that it is almost second nature to us to utilize conscious language in our daily lives.

Now, in the new consciousness, our intent is becoming even more of a factor in creation. That means that our own vibrational frequency, our own personal intent, will be the signature way in which we communicate with the Universe for the purpose of co-creation. Of course we will still use conscious language, but the focus will shift from using the exact metaphysically perfect words in every case, to radiating our pure intentions to the Universe through authenticity and deep awareness.

The reason for this shift in emphasis from words to intentions is because our relationship to the language of the past is changing as we continue to evolve into the higher dimensional realities. We may actually have evolved past the vibration of some words from language to the point that we don't need to use them or may not even recognize them consciously anymore.

I'll share an example with you. I was having dinner with an old friend of mine a couple of years ago and during the course of our conversation, he was talking about an old colleague as being "vindictive." I was rather surprised as I reached into my consciousness to recall that particular word and realized that I couldn't quite grasp it. It was like running into someone from my past from 30 years ago and not being able to remember their name or where I knew them from. The word was vaguely familiar, and of course, I knew that I had known exactly what it meant, but it just escaped me during that conversation.

It later occurred to me that the energy of the word "vindictive" was just no longer vibrating at my same frequency. I could no longer relate to it the way I could with many common words that I have known and used for my entire life. So in evolving beyond the energy of a word, we can find that we evolve beyond the word itself.

In a way, we are also adapting new intent to some old language. For example, the word "love" has been used to mean a variety of things within the context of humanity. We've used terms such as *real* love, *true* love, or *unconditional* love to clarify the kind of love that matches our intent.

Then we evolved to a place with the word "love" where we experience all love as unconditional love and no other kind of love is actually love at all. In other words, love is love, and any labeling of it beyond that dilutes its meaning.

Now, as we operate more in the higher dimensional realities, we are beginning to experience a new higher vibration of this intent, which we really don't have words for yet. So we may begin to use phrases like, "I *more* than love you." This is an attempt to fit our higher dimensional reality into the language we have been so familiar with, but not having it quite fit the way it used to.

I've included this guidance about language and intention because it is important to understand that the way we communicate with each other and the world around us is changing along with our vibration, particularly as we function more on an intuitive level of knowing. At times, it's not necessary to scrutinize every possible metaphysical meaning of a word or phrase to convey intent. Particularly as we function in between dimensional realities, we may find that we go back and forth between using old consciousness language, and new consciousness intent. It feels to me at times like speaking a sort of hybrid language, if you will.

You will find even within the context of this book that I am less concerned with using precise "correct" wording in accordance with metaphysical principles and more concerned with conveying intent by guiding your conscious awareness. I've experienced our communication tools evolving as rapidly as we are, and you may discover the same.

"The truth is that we are infinite beings evolving rapidly into ascension."

CHAPTER NINETEEN

EXPANDING INTO ASCENSION

It's been a long-held belief that we are somehow finite beings and that once we are born and reach a certain middle age, that we begin a slow decline culminating to our eventual end. This is an illusion that is becoming more understood as such as we anchor ourselves in the higher dimensional realities. The truth is that we are infinite beings evolving rapidly into ascension.

I've had many mentors in this lifetime, and most of them have held some sort of perspective on the relationship of past, present, parallel, and future lives. It wasn't until I started to work in-depth with the guidance I received while developing Quantum Prayer that I was able to experience my infinite nature within the context of quantum reality. I'll never forget an early mentor of mine saying, as I approached the end of this incarnation, that I would already be preparing for what came next. At the time, I knew what he meant by that, but I had only thought of it then in terms of preparing for something in the future.

I now realize that I have always been in the process of preparing, and not just for what comes next. I was not yet aware, as I am now, that we are always creating and we are always a creation in process. We never end, in fact, but we are always evolving. By being aware of our true infinite nature, we can apply all creative principles to every life-space we have ever had or will have because they are all happening at once. Whatever we create for ourselves now, affects every one of those life-spaces, culminating in this process of expanding into ascension at an increasingly rapid pace.

We are moving closer and closer toward the vibration of Heaven on Earth. Instead of leaving earth and going to heaven, we are inviting heaven to co-create our new earth in its likeness. We are quickly leaving behind all that no longer serves us and embracing the luxury of Universal Law and conscious evolution. It really is a great time to be alive.

> "…you may find yourself expanding to exemplify a kind of 'living prayer.' When this occurs, you are operating in the quantum realms where all things are possible, instantly."

CHAPTER TWENTY

ACCESSING YOU

It has been a privilege to introduce you to Quantum Prayer, to share with you my own story and my experiences with this guidance, and to impart to you a vision of co-creation for a new Heaven on Earth. It is my sincere wish that this work assist you in your evolutionary process in accordance with your own highest good.

There is much more to share in the way of Quantum Prayer, but for now I will leave you with some parting guidance on accessing *you* through the awareness of your infinite nature, and using this awareness to create with intention.

There are many ways to access through awareness, but the one I use most frequently is a kind of guided meditation. When I'm working alone, this is a self-guided meditation, which you can do as well. The key is to stay focused on your awareness of your infinite self and your specific intentions. Once you've experienced this level of conscious creation, it may become easier to access each time. You may find yourself proportionately more and more in the higher dimensional realities, even outside of a meditative practice. In other words, you may find yourself expanding to exemplify a kind of "living prayer." When this occurs, you are operating in the quantum realms where all things are possible, instantly.

This is the very simple and basic meditation that anyone can easily use at any time. I recommend you start in a quiet place where you can relax, close your eyes, and focus. With some practice, you will be able to do this under any circumstance. I share this with you now in the highest vibrations of infinite love, peace, and joy.

A Basic Quantum Prayer Meditation

Bring into your mind's eye the image of a small seed of light. This seed of light is held in the palm of your hand. This seed of light is the original seed of *you*. This seed of you is pure, divine love and light, and it holds your original, perfect, divine blueprint. Continue to hold it freely in the palm of your hand. At the same time, bring into your awareness all of your incarnations, past, present, parallel, and future. Become aware of every aspect of you, every unique expression of you in every life-space, universe, galaxy, and in all of creation. Every part of you that has ever existed, every particle and cell of your every incarnation is now in your awareness all at once.

Place your intentions for whatever it is that you are wishing to create for yourself, whether it be healing, abundance, love, joy, etc., inside your seed of light and let that original seed of you expand infinitely through your awareness of every incarnation, aspect, and unique expression of you. Direct your seed of light to imbue your intention into every life-space, clearing out and overwriting anything and everything that is not in harmony with your intention. Reset the manifestation of you to vibrate at the frequency of your intent while simultaneously retaining the divine light and truth of all life lessons, wisdom, and evolutionary progress in accordance with your highest good. See that intent manifest in every incarnation, every life-space, every conceivable aspect and expression of you. Experience your self in the vibration of your intent for as long as you wish.

(end of meditation)

At first, I often used this kind of meditation when in bed at night just before falling asleep. It's a great time to practice awareness without the distractions of the world around you. However, I did reach a point where it didn't matter where I was or what was going on around me. I could stay in this state of conscious awareness and creation unencumbered. May you be blessed with the same and more in your own quest for Heaven on Earth.

A SPECIAL NOTE FROM SUSANA

"We're living a transition into a new era, with a new energy, new rules, and new consciousness. Things that have served humanity in past centuries seem to be different now and we are getting into new dimensions of consciousness. The power of positive thoughts can now be scientifically proven and our story is a testament to that. We can create our life with our daily thoughts and, if we think and act with love, the Universe will reflect that back to us. When we become aware of this, it's a very precious gift to ourselves and humanity."

—**Susana**

ABOUT THE AUTHOR

Along his journey, **Joshua Kai** has worked with many mentors, metaphysical modalities, and healing philosophies that have been his constant companions and teachers for years. In committing to his own self mastery and evolutionary progress, Joshua discovered himself accessing his true, authentic self in ways he could not have readily imagined earlier in life. With a desire to serve humanity and no attachment to what that might look like, Joshua found himself in the midst of an inspiring life with increasing conscious awareness and many gifts to share. Joshua is now an author, Naturopathic Doctor, and Spiritual Teacher dedicated to working with people around the world to achieve their best life possible by honoring and encouraging self mastery, wisdom, and intuition while supporting optimal health and wellness goals with enlightened information and perspective.

"Even the smallest shift in perspective can bring about the greatest healing." —Dr. Joshua Kai, ND

JOIN THE QUANTUM PRAYER MOVEMENT

If you would like to add your name to the **official Quantum Prayer list,** please send us your name and email address to Joshua@MakaioLight.com . You will be added to the list and included in Dr. Kai's regular Quantum Prayer practice and will also receive updates on any additional opportunities.

~

To find out more about Dr. Kai's revolutionary partnership program with Dr. Gerda Edwards, **Rebuilding Health from Chronic Illness**, visit www.MakaioLight.com or email us at Joshua@MakaioLight.com .

~

To schedule an appointment for a Reconnective Healing® session by distance, or to find out more about Reconnective Healing® or The Reconnection® visit www.MakaioLight.com or email us at Joshua@MakaioLight.com

---

[i] Sheila Cash, a Teacher on the Evolution of Consciousness, can be found at www.SheilaCash.com (coming in 2015)

[ii] The Unique Nutritional Profile™ is owned by and exclusively used by Dr. Joshua Kai, ND and Dr. Gerda Edwards, PhD, DNM in their partnership programs on *Rebuilding Health From Chronic Illness*. More information can be found at www.MakaioLight.com

[iii] Gary Zukav, "Spiritual Partnership: The Journey to Authentic Power." See also http://seatofthesoul.com/books/spiritual-partnership/

Made in the USA
Middletown, DE
22 February 2015